Ultimate FACTIVITY Collection

Find out all about *Star Wars Rebels*™ with fun, fascinating activities that help you learn as you play. All the activities can be done right on the page—you just need a few colored pencils and some imagination!

Contents

Find out about the rebel crew of the *Ghost* and their battle against the Empire. Help Ezra with his Jedi training, draw graffiti with Sabine, and paint the *Ghost*!

Discover how the terrible Empire has conquered the galaxy with its powerful army. Complete a sticker jigsaw of the fearsome AT-DP and write an Imperial report.

The Imperial army has occupied the rebels' planet of Lothal. Complete a guide to the planet, ruin an Imperial poster, and design a stylish new speeder bike!

The rebels take the fight to the Empire! Complete a comic book of a high-speed chase, help the rebels save some Wookiees, and create your own lightsaber.

This book belongs to:

✏ _____

The Force

The Force is a powerful and mysterious energy. It has two sides— light and dark. Heroes use the light side, while villains exploit the dark side.

Ezra

Ezra is the youngest of the rebels. He grew up on Lothal. Ezra's parents vanished many years ago, and since then he has been alone.

The evil Empire rules the galaxy, but there are some who are brave enough to stand up to it. On the planet Lothal, a small team of rebels have joined forces to battle against the Empire. They must fight to free their world!

Find the **stickers** at the back of the book.

Hera

Hera is a master starship pilot. Her super-fast reflexes and excellent flying skills make her more than a match for Imperial pilots.

Zeb

Zeb is a strong, tough fighter from the planet Lasan. He only wants one thing—to bash Imperial stormtroopers.

Kanan

Brave Kanan is a Jedi. The Jedi were noble guardians who were nearly wiped out by the Empire. He is training Ezra to become a Jedi, too.

Chopper

Chopper is a cranky old droid. He complains all the time and plays pranks on everyone, but he is the only one who can keep the *Ghost* running.

Sabine

Sabine is a young warrior from Mandalore. She is feisty and bold, and she loves two things: painting and blowing things up!

The *Ghost*

The *Ghost* is Hera's ship. It looks like a normal space freighter, but it is actually a fast, tough battleship.

Jedi Training
Fill in the missing words

Kanan must train Ezra in the ways of the Force if he is to become a Jedi. The Force is a mysterious energy field that gives Jedi their powers. Jedi use the light side of the Force to protect the innocent and battle against evil.

Lonely teacher

Kanan has spent years hiding his Jedi abilities from the Empire. Teaching Ezra will help Kanan to remember his own Jedi training.

Read about Ezra's Jedi training, then fill in the missing words opposite.

Side by side

Ezra and Kanan fight against the Empire as Master and Padawan. Although Ezra has powerful Force abilities, he is not a Jedi yet.

Ways of the Force

A Holocron is a training device that Jedi use to store information. Only someone who feels the Force can open one. Ezra opens Kanan's Holocron, showing that he can sense the Force.

Learning the hard way

There are no shortcuts to becoming a Jedi. Ezra must learn to control his emotions and be patient. If he is easily frustrated, he risks falling short of his goal.

BECOMING A JEDI

Find the **sticker** at the back of the book.

1 Jedi use the ✎ _____ side of the Force to battle evil.

2 A ✎ _____ is an object that Jedi use to store information.

3 Only someone who feels the ✎ _____ can open a holocron.

4 To become a Jedi, Ezra must learn to control his ✎ _____ .

5 Ezra and Kanan battle the Empire as Master and ✎ _____ .

Find the **answers** on page 97.

The *Ghost*

Give the *Ghost* a new paint job

The *Ghost* is far more than just a ship. It is the rebels' home, transportation, and battleship. The *Ghost* is tough and fast, and its special systems mean that it can often sneak past the Empire's ships without being detected!

Read about the *Ghost*, then color in the outline to give it a new paint job.

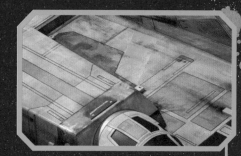

Painted hull
Unlike the boring gray color of Imperial ships, the *Ghost* is painted with bright colors.

The *Phantom*
The *Ghost* has a smaller shuttle craft named the *Phantom*. The *Phantom* docks with the rear of the ship when not flying separate missions.

Hera Syndulla
Hera is the captain of the *Ghost*. This feisty Twi'lek freedom fighter uses her ship to carry the rebels on their missions. She can outfly even the best Imperial pilots!

The cockpit
The *Ghost*'s cockpit has space for four of the rebels to sit together. In front of the cockpit is the nose gun turret.

Will you paint the Ghost **dark** colors for camouflage, or **bright** colors?

Remember to color in the **Ghost**'s cockpit!

Rebel Weapons

Match the weapon to its owner

The rebels are all fighting the same enemy, but they have a variety of fighting styles and use very different weapons. Some weapons are better in close combat and others for long-range battles, but all help in the fight against the Empire.

Read about the weapons, then work out which one belongs to each rebel and draw it in their hands.

Zeb's weapon is perfect for **close combat**.

Zeb

Lasat warrior Zeb can use his weapon to blast enemies from a distance, or turn it into a staff and zap his targets with electric shocks.

Weapons

Blaster pistols

These custom-painted blaster pistols reflect the creative flair of their owner. Plus they are fast, reliable, and capable of super-precise shooting.

Lightsaber

Lightsabers are the traditional weapons of Jedi Knights. Now that the very few surviving Jedi are in hiding from the Empire, it is very dangerous to be caught with one.

Bo-rifle

The powerful bo-rifle is used only by Lasats. It can easily transform from a rifle into an electrified fighting staff.

*Kanan's weapon is perfect for a **Jedi**.*

*Sabine has a weapon in **each hand**.*

Kanan

Kanan keeps his Jedi identity hidden. He has to keep his weapon in a secret compartment on board the *Ghost* so that no one discovers who he really is.

Find the **answers** on page 97.

Sabine

Sabine has decorated her weapons so they are as colorful as she is. But looks can be deceiving—there is nothing pretty about the damage they can do.

Chopper
Draw an astromech droid

C1-10P—or "Chopper," as he is better known—is a type of robot called an astromech droid. Chopper works with the rebels and is the mechanic on Hera's ship, the *Ghost*. He is old and grumpy, but he gets things done—eventually!

Read about Chopper and then create your own astromech droid.

Electroshock prod

He may have tons of built-in gadgets, but Chopper's personal favorite is his electroshock prod. If his enemies get too close, they are in for a nasty surprise!

Handy tools

Chopper has three grasping arms: two that extend from his head and a handy extra one that tucks away neatly inside his body when not in use.

Rocket booster

Chopper's impressive rocket booster can help him distract Imperials. Plus it is perfect for escaping from tight spots.

Give your droid some useful **extra parts**.

Is your droid **rusty** and **old** or **shiny** and **new**?

Remember to draw in your droid's **head**!

My astromech droid is named:

Zeb Orrelios

Complete the sticker jigsaw

Garazeb "Zeb" Orrelios is a muscly rebel who really hates the Empire. His homeworld, Lasan, was destroyed by Imperial troops. Zeb may seem tough and grouchy, but he does have a sensitive side, too.

Learn about Zeb, then complete the sticker jigsaw.

Plan of action

Zeb prefers bold mission plans. He doesn't like sneaking around, as it means there is less chance of fighting someone!

Bo-rifle battles

Zeb loves fighting Imperial soldiers. His honor guard training means that the stormtroopers on Lothal don't stand a chance against him!

Honorable warrior

Zeb was once an honor guard on Lasan. This means he was one of the strongest and bravest of all the warriors on his planet.

Find the **stickers** at the back of the book.

Bo-rifle

Zeb's weapon can quickly switch from being a rifle into an electrified fighting staff.

Fighting staff mode

In fighting staff mode, Zeb's bo-rifle can take out stormtroopers with ease. One prod and they will be out cold for hours!

Powerful legs

Zeb is a Lasat. Lasats can run much faster and jump much higher than humans.

Gripping feet

Zeb can use his feet like they are another pair of hands. He can grab objects or climb up things with them.

Find the **answers** on page 97.

Artistic Flair
Design a graffiti tag

Sabine Wren is a tough explosives expert, but she is also hooked on creating graffiti art. She has a very dangerous habit of leaving her personal graffiti symbol, known as a tag, on Imperial property!

Read about Sabine's artistic skills and then design your own tag.

Colorful style
Even Sabine's hair is brightly colored.

Leaving her mark
Sabine knows that her artwork could get her into trouble, but she doesn't care. It's her way of showing the Empire that she's not afraid to stand up to it.

Rebel tag
The starbird symbol is the mark of the rebels. Sabine makes sure it is always clear for the Imperial guards to see!

Trusty airbrushes
There's always an airbrush or two stashed in Sabine's gear. She's ready to paint on walls, Imperial vehicles, and, if she's fast, even an unconscious stormtrooper!

Customized armor
Sabine's knee-guards are often splattered with paint.

Decide if you want your tag to be **words** or **pictures**.

Will your design be **big and bold** or small and harder to spot?

Your tag could be any **color** you like!

Chapter 1 Challenge
Test your knowledge of Chapter 1

Answer each question. If you need help, look back through the section.

Now you have finished the first chapter of the book, take the Challenge to find out if you are a rebel expert!

1. Find the sticker that best matches the description:

This feisty rebel is the Captain of the _Ghost_.

2. How many grasping arms does Chopper have?

Three ◯   **Five** ◯   **Six** ◯

3. Zeb's weapon of choice is a bo-rifle.

True ◯   **False** ◯

4. What is this Jedi's name? ✎ _____

5. Sabine likes to graffiti a starbird symbol onto ✎ _____ property.

Find the **answers** on page 97.

Now you have finished the Challenge, fill this scene with your extra stickers!

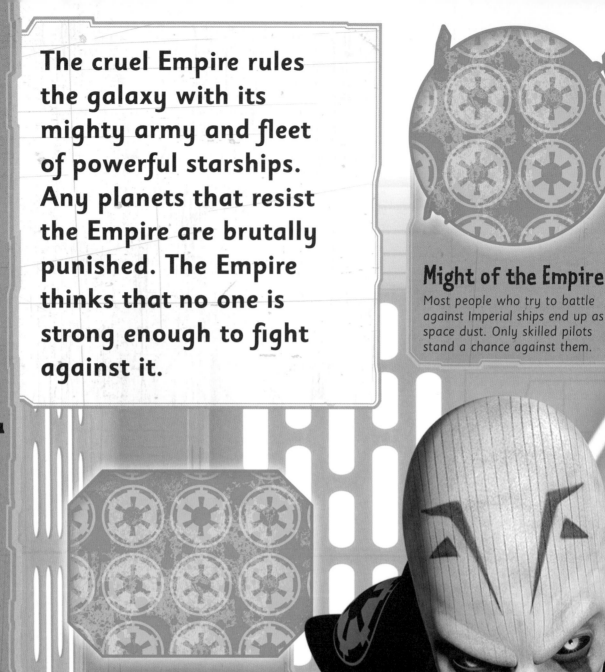

The cruel Empire rules the galaxy with its mighty army and fleet of powerful starships. Any planets that resist the Empire are brutally punished. The Empire thinks that no one is strong enough to fight against it.

CHAPTER 2 ● The Empire

Might of the Empire

Most people who try to battle against Imperial ships end up as space dust. Only skilled pilots stand a chance against them.

Agent Kallus

Ruthless Agent Kallus is a member of the Imperial secret police. He loves nothing more than wiping out rebels.

Find the **stickers** at the back of the book.

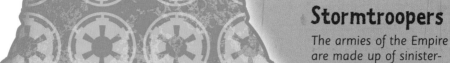

Stormtroopers

The armies of the Empire are made up of sinister-looking stormtroopers. These soldiers follow orders without question.

Star Destroyer

Star Destroyers are among the most powerful ships in the galaxy. They can blast entire cities into ash!

Aresko and Grint

These two Imperial officers serve the Empire on Lothal. They are mean and cold-hearted, and care only about themselves.

Imperial pilots

Imperial pilots are arrogant and ruthless warriors. They think that their flying skills are unbeatable.

The Inquisitor

The scary Inquisitor uses the dark side of the Force to hunt for Jedi. When he finds one, he destroys them.

For the Empire!

Identify the Imperial officers

The Empire's most loyal soldiers are the officers of the Imperial army. Imperial officers are usually cruel bullies. They only care about serving the Empire, and they ignore all of the awful suffering that it causes.

Read about the Imperial officers, then use the clues to identify each officer.

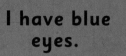

I have blue eyes.

I look after property.

Farmers are scared of me.

Find the **stickers** at the back of the book.

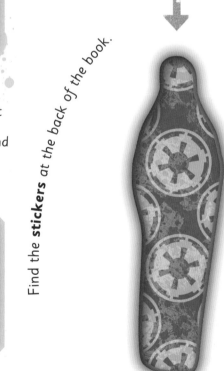

Grint

Taskmaster Grint is strong, but not very smart. Mostly he just does what Aresko tells him. He enjoys bullying people who are smaller than him.

Kallus

Agent Kallus cares only about one thing: destroying rebels. He is a smart commander and a frightening warrior.

Aresko

Commandant Aresko thinks he is smarter than he really is. He does not care about the people of Lothal, but enjoys having power over them.

Lyste

Supply Master Lyste is in charge of Imperial property on Lothal. When farmers refuse to move out, he takes them prisoner and destroys their farms.

1 My name is:

_____

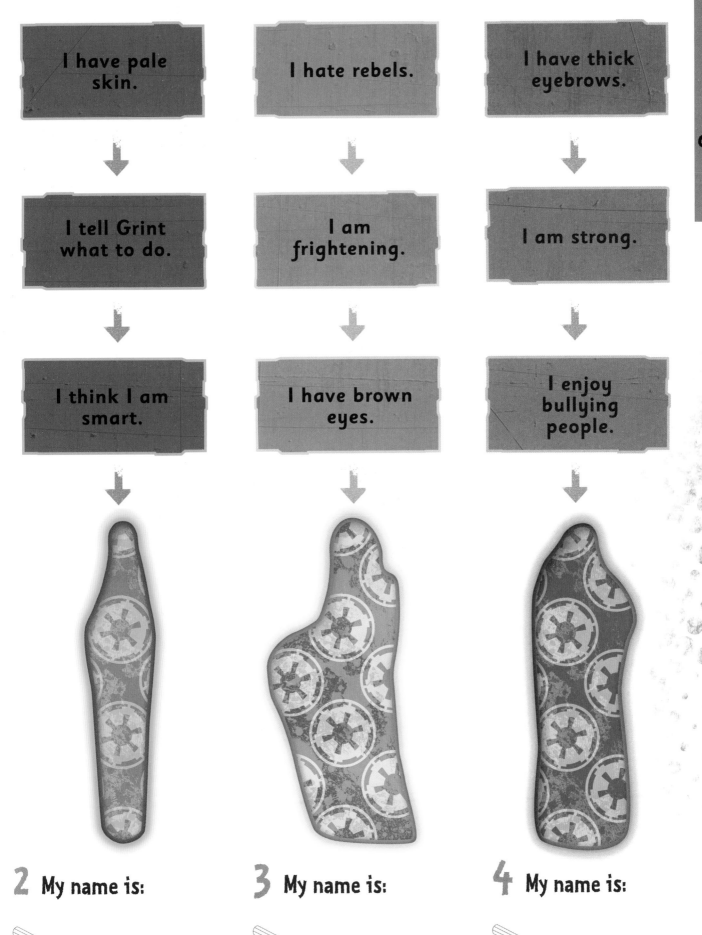

I have pale skin.

↓

I tell Grint what to do.

↓

I think I am smart.

↓

2 My name is:

✎ _____

I hate rebels.

↓

I am frightening.

↓

I have brown eyes.

↓

3 My name is:

✎ _____

I have thick eyebrows.

↓

I am strong.

↓

I enjoy bullying people.

↓

4 My name is:

✎ _____

Find the **answers** on page 97.

Agent Kallus

Design new armor

Dangerous Agent Kallus is a highly trained Empire operative, and a formidable foe of the rebels. Skilled in both piloting vehicles and fighting on the ground, Kallus will stop at nothing to track down his prey.

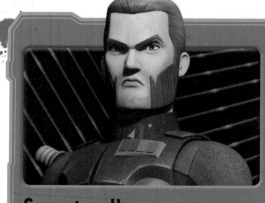

Secret police

Agent Kallus is ambitious and works tirelessly for the Imperial Security Bureau, the Empire's secret police. He scours Lothal for any signs of resistance and ruthlessly stamps them out.

Read about Agent Kallus's armor, then design and draw your own new version for him to wear.

Custom armor

Kallus's custom-made armor can withstand the hardest of blows in hand-to-hand combat. It is also lightweight, allowing him to be swift and flexible.

Extra plate reinforces helmet

Built-in comlink communication

Side panels guard face and neck

ISB helmet

This sturdy Imperial Security Bureau helmet is designed for riot control and heavy combat situations. The style shows that the owner is an agent.

Stolen Lasat bo-rifle

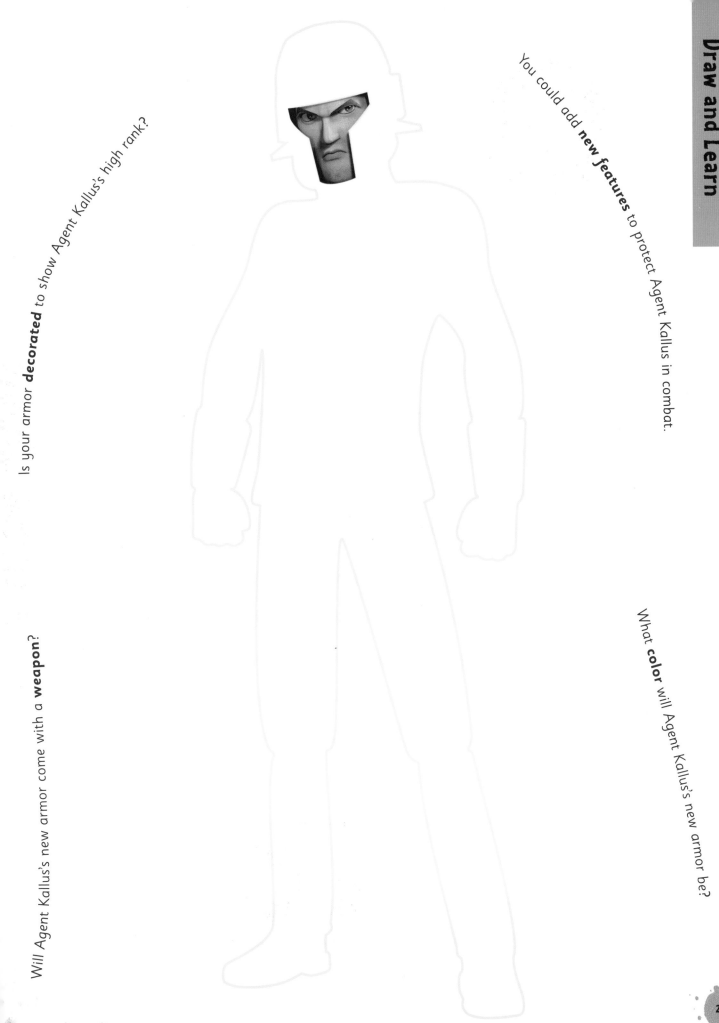

You could add **new features** to protect Agent Kallus in combat.

Is your armor **decorated** to show Agent Kallus's high rank?

What **color** will Agent Kallus's new armor be?

Will Agent Kallus's new armor come with a **weapon**?

AT-DP

Complete the sticker jigsaw

AT-DPs (All Terrain Defense Pods) are used by the Empire to frighten would-be rebels and keep public order. These mighty walking vehicles patrol the streets of Lothal and hunt for suspicious activity during scouting missions.

Read about the AT-DP vehicle, then use stickers to complete the jigsaw.

Laser cannon

Most Lothal citizens quake in their boots when they see this front-facing heavy laser cannon on the horizon.

Cockpit

The AT-DP's cockpit can usually hold two pilots. The one sitting in front steers the vehicle, and the second pilot behind is in charge of firing the cannon.

Find the **stickers** at the back of the book.

Hide and seek

Nighttime on Lothal holds no difficulties for AT-DPs: their bright spotlights can quickly find other vehicles lurking in the shadows.

Stabilizer pad

The AT-DP is so tall that it can be hard to maintain balance. Each leg has a stabilizer pad that senses the terrain below, to help keep the vehicle upright.

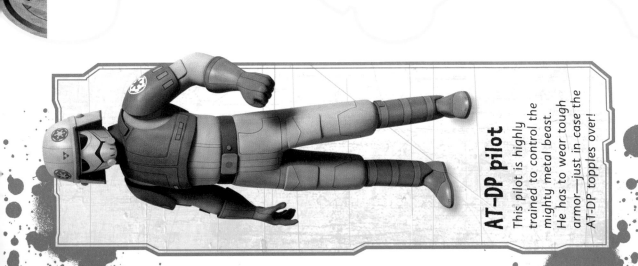

AT-DP pilot

This pilot is highly trained to control the mighty metal beast. He has to wear tough armor—just in case the AT-DP topples over!

Battling the Rebels
Write Agent Kallus's mission report

The rebels on Lothal have begun to cause serious problems for the Empire. Important Imperial bases have been destroyed and valuable technology has been stolen. Agent Kallus now has only one job—to track down the rebels and destroy them!

Read about one of Agent Kallus's battles, then write his report about it.

1 The rebels **break into a docking bay** on the planet Garel, and **steal** an important shipment of **disruptor rifles**.

2 The rebels manage to blast off from the planet and **fly back to Lothal** with their valuable cargo.

3 The rebels try to **sell the weapons** to a gangster named **Cikatro Vizago**, but the Empire has followed them!

4 The Empire **attacks the rebels**. Agent Kallus leads AT-DP walkers and stormtroopers into battle.

5 Agent Kallus uses his bo-rifle to take on Zeb in close combat. He manages to **defeat Zeb** and is about to finish him off!

6 **Ezra** uses the **Force** to throw Agent Kallus through the air. The **rebels escape**—Agent Kallus has **failed**.

IMPERIAL OFFICER MISSION REPORT

REPORT LOGGED BY: AGENT KALLUS

Mission target:

_____

Mission result:

_____

Mission analysis: _____

_____

_____

_____

_____

_____

_____

_____

Kallus will have to **explain what happened** in the mission and **why**.

Find the **sticker** of Agent Kallus at the back of the book.

Remember to write the report from **Agent Kallus**'s point of view.

Imperial Ships
Complete the pictures

The Imperial fleet is the most powerful space force in the galaxy. Its mighty Star Destroyers can easily smash any opposition, while swarms of TIE fighters overwhelm any ships that try to attack or escape.

Find the stickers of the missing halves of these Imperial ships to complete them.

Freighters have pointed noses.

Freighter

Imperial freighters are used to carry cargoes that are too valuable for normal freighters. They are heavily

Jail break

Freighters often transport prisoners of the Empire to prison planets or labor camps. These missions make them an important target for the rebels.

Cockpit view

The large window in the cockpit gives TIE fighter pilots a good view. Scopes in the cockpit show system status and target information.

TIE fighters have two wings with solar panels on.

TIE fighter

The Empire uses small, one-pilot TIE fighters to shoot down enemy ships, and to support Imperial ground troops.

The bridge

The bridge is a Star Destroyer's command center. From here, the ship's officers can scan nearby space and give orders in battle.

Star Destroyers are long and dagger-shaped.

Star Destroyer

1,600 meters long, and with a crew of more than 40,000 people, a Star Destroyer is a giant mobile city. Its turbolaser cannons can blast other ships into flaming wreckage.

Find the **stickers** at the back of the book.

The Inquisitor

Draw your own Inquisitor

The Inquisitor is a sinister servant of the Empire. He is trained to track down and destroy Jedi. The dark side gives him special abilities and makes him a powerful warrior, and he often uses it to scare his enemies.

Read about the Inquisitor. Then fill in the outline opposite to draw your own.

Lightsaber

This lightsaber has several different modes. Its spinning blades are designed to destroy Jedi!

Dark armor

The Inquisitor wears an unusual suit of armor, with a large collar and wide shoulder guards.

Terrifying tattoos

Red is the color of anger, and of the dark side. The Inquisitor's red tattoos show that he is strong with the dark side of the Force.

Dark side eyes

If someone turns to the dark side, it starts to change how they look. Over time, their eyes become red and yellow!

Pau'an fangs

The Inquisitor is a Pau'an. Pau'ans' sharp teeth make them look scary, and allow them to chew their favorite food—raw meat!

Use **colors** to create your own dark side **tattoos**.

Does your Inquisitor have **scary teeth**?

Use this outline to **draw** your own **Inquisitor**.

Chapter 2 Challenge

Test your knowledge of Chapter 2

Answer each question. If you need help, look back through the section.

Now you have finished the second chapter of the book, take the Challenge to find out if you know all about the Empire!

1. Find the sticker that best matches the description:

This sturdy helmet is designed for riot control and heavy combat.

2. What color are the Inquisitor's tattoos?

Black ◯   **Green** ◯   **Red** ◯

3. TIE fighters are used to transport Imperial prisoners.

True ◯   **False** ◯

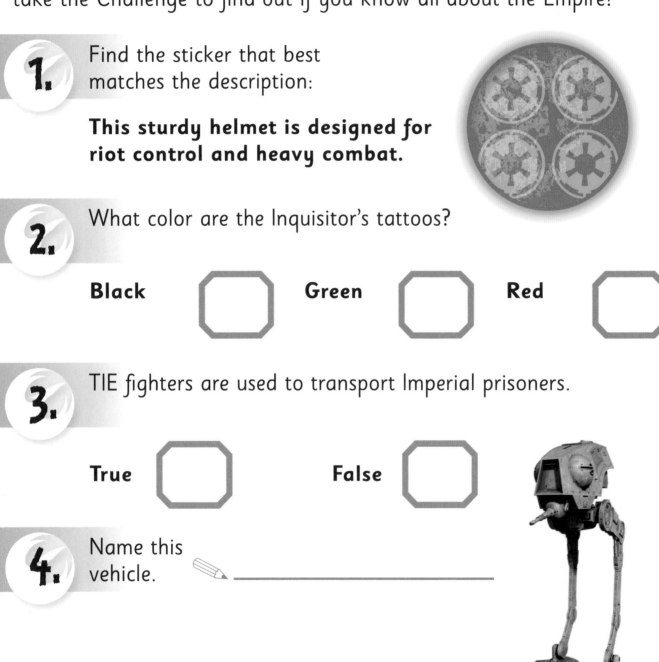

4. Name this vehicle. ✏ _____

5. A ✏ _____ has a crew of more than 40,000 people.

Find the **answers** on page 97.

Now you have finished the Challenge, fill this scene with your extra stickers!

Lothal

Lothal has a warm climate, with clear shallow seas, wide grassy plains, and rocky mountains.

Fighting the Empire

Lothal has become the site of a fierce battle between the Empire and rebels. The streets are sometimes dangerous.

The planet Lothal used to be a nice place to live. But now the Empire's rule is very harsh and the people suffer a lot. Crime, hunger, and hard labor are part of everyday life. Most Lothal citizens just try to stay out of the Empire's way.

Find the **stickers** at the back of the book.

Capital City

Capital City is the biggest city on Lothal. The massive Imperial Complex looms above the streets and factories.

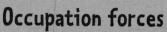

Occupation forces

Lothal is valuable to the Empire, so it keeps a strong force on the planet. Imperial troops and vehicles are everywhere.

Burning farms

Smoke on the horizon is becoming a common sight on Lothal. The Empire burns farms to make space for mines and factories.

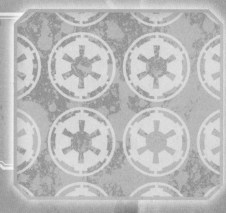

Lothal wildlife

Lothal has some unique wildlife. Loth-cats are predators that live on the planet's grassy plains.

The Broken Horn

The Broken Horn, led by Cikatro Vizago, is the biggest criminal gang on Lothal. It smuggles weapons and illegal goods.

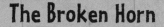

Rebel speeders

Lothal is a big place, and there aren't many roads. To get around fast, a speeder bike is a vital piece of equipment.

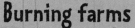
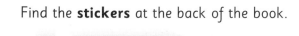

Guide to Lothal

Identify the locations

Ezra has spent years exploring Lothal and dodging the Imperial forces. He knows the best hiding places, the best spots to take things from the Empire—and the areas that are best avoided!

Ezra has lived on Lothal his whole life.

Read about these places, then find the stickers of them.

Ezra's Guide

Capital City

This city is crowded and full of grimy factories. It's a great place to steal from the Empire, but it can be dangerous!

Imperial base

I try to steer clear of Imperial bases. They are always heavily guarded and full of stormtroopers.

Rocky outcrops

These outcrops are a perfect place for me to hide things, but it is easy to get lost. The Empire usually avoids them.

My tower

This rusty old tower doesn't look like much, but it is safe, and I can keep an eye on the Empire from here.

Find the **stickers** at the back of the book.

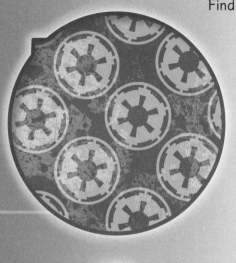

1 This place is strongly guarded by lots of Imperial troops.

This location is:

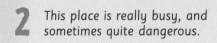
_____

2 This place is really busy, and sometimes quite dangerous.

This location is:

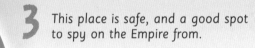
_____

3 This place is safe, and a good spot to spy on the Empire from.

This location is:

_____

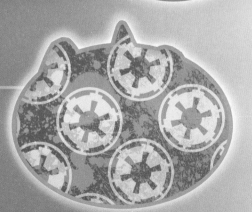

4 This is a great place to hide things that I've taken.

This location is:

_____

Find the **answers** on page 97.

Imperial Vehicles

Identify the vehicles

To keep control over all of Lothal, the Empire uses its powerful vehicles. They are supposed to look menacing to scare the locals, but these ugly war machines don't frighten the rebels!

Read about the Imperial vehicles, then use the clues to choose the right sticker.

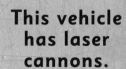
This vehicle has laser cannons.

This vehicle is speedy.

This vehicle can fly.

Speeder bike

Speeder bikes are light and super-fast. They are used to hunt down escaping rebels, and to scout over long distances.

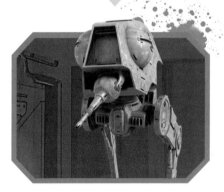

AT-DP

These heavy, armored walking machines have a powerful laser cannon. Their long legs mean they can run very fast.

TIE fighter

Speedy TIE fighters are designed to fight in space, but they can fly through the air, too. They blast things with their laser cannons.

ITT

ITTs are built to carry stormtroopers. They have heavy armor, which makes them very tough, but they are also slow.

1 The vehicle is:

✏ _____

This vehicle looks blocky.

⬇

This vehicle is slow.

⬇

This vehicle transports stormtroopers.

⬇

This vehicle has armor.

⬇

This vehicle has a laser cannon.

⬇

This vehicle has legs.

⬇

This vehicle is not very heavy.

⬇

This vehicle has one pilot.

⬇

This vehicle is super-fast.

⬇

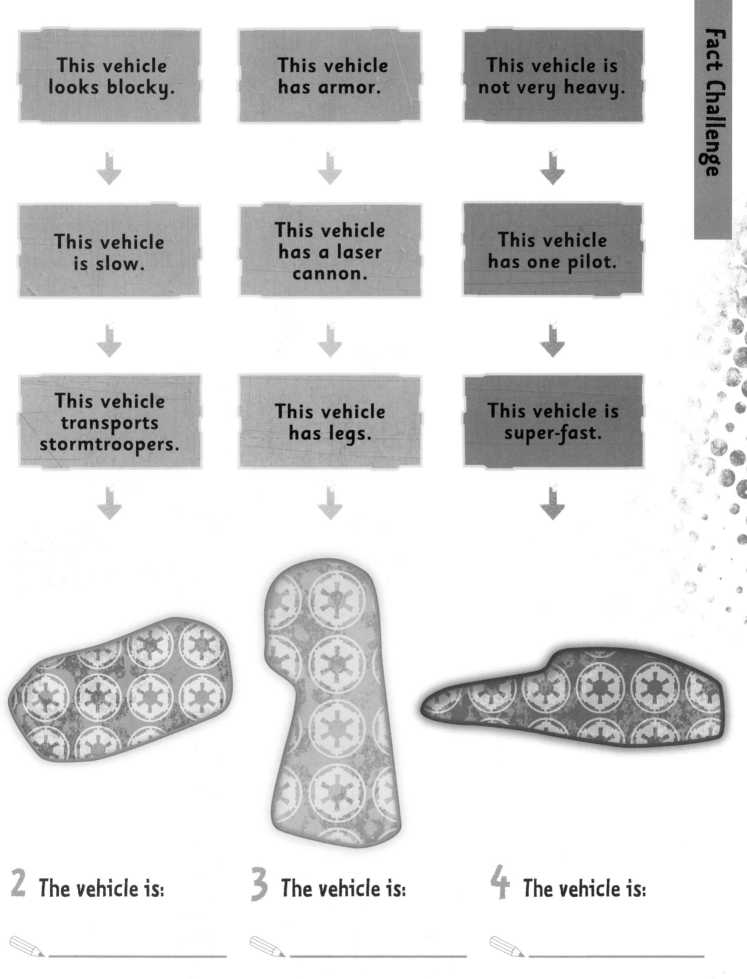

2 The vehicle is:

✎ _____

3 The vehicle is:

✎ _____

4 The vehicle is:

✎ _____

Find the **answers** on page 97.

39

Cikatro Vizago
Create new bodyguards

The Empire has made many luxury items illegal on Lothal. Gangsters like Cikatro Vizago have moved in to take advantage of this. They offer to smuggle illegal things past the Empire—for a price.

Learn about Vizago and his bodyguards, then create some new ones!

The broken horn

Vizago is not embarrassed that one of his horns is broken—he has named his gang and his ship after it!

Computer brain feels no pity or mercy

Heavy blaster rifle

Lord of crime

Vizago is the criminal boss on Lothal. His gang, the Broken Horn, controls illegal shipments of weapons and luxury goods. For Vizago, business is all that matters.

Vizago's bodyguards

Vizago has a crew of IG-RM thug droids. These act as his bodyguards. They are not very smart, but they are strong, which is helpful for moving heavy shipments around.

Information dealer

Vizago knows about everything that happens on Lothal. The rebels come to him for information, but they definitely don't trust him!

You should draw **two guards**, one **either side** of Vizago.

What **kind** of bodyguards do you think **Vizago** would want?

Name Vizago's new bodyguards:

Capital City
Help Zeb to escape!

Capital City is the most important place on Lothal. It is a center of industry, business, and Imperial power. The rebels must be careful when they go to Capital City, as the Imperials are always on the lookout for trouble!

Make your way through the maze, getting past trouble as you go. Add stickers as you make it through!

On the run
Zeb has been spotted! He will need to work his way through the winding streets and alleyways, and try not to get caught by the Empire!

START

The market
The market is a busy place, full of traders trying to sell food. Zeb must try to blend in with the crowd—there are stormtroopers everywhere!

Boom!
Sabine has come to help Zeb! She has set off an explosion to distract the stormtroopers. In the confusion, Zeb should be able to slip past unseen.

Find the **stickers** at the back of the book.

Congratulations!

Zeb has managed to get past the Empire's troops. Hera swoops in and picks him up in the *Ghost*, and the rebels fly to safety!

FINISH

Code Red!

The Imperials have called in a Code Red! This means that they are under attack. Zeb will have to be careful, as they will be looking even harder for him now!

Dark alleyways

Capital City is a maze of narrow alleyways. It is easy to get lost, but it is also easy to hide. Zeb can stay in a dark doorway while the stormtroopers run past.

Stormtrooper trouble

Zeb has managed to come this far without fighting, but now he will have to clear a path using his bo-rifle. These stormtroopers will never know what hit them!

Find the **answers** on page 97.

43

Speeder Bikes

Design your own speeder bike

Speeder bikes are a great way of getting around fast! There are lots of different kinds. Sabine, Kanan, and Ezra all have their own speeder bikes, and love nothing more than a high-speed ride across the plains of Lothal!

Find out about these speeder bikes, then use them to design your own.

Rangefinder helps with high-speed driving

Speed and altitude controls

Compact engine

Sabine's speeder bike

This speeder bike is an unusual shape. It is called a jumpspeeder, and Sabine controls it using the big pedals on the front.

Pedals control direction

Kanan's speeder bike

This speeder bike is called a Joben T-85. This type is not very common on Lothal, but Kanan loves its smooth lines and powerful engines.

Handlebars

Repulsor generator

Acceleration pedal

Ezra's speeder bike

Imperial speeder bikes are not designed to look pretty—they're built for speed and firepower. Ezra stole this one, then customized it with his favorite colors!

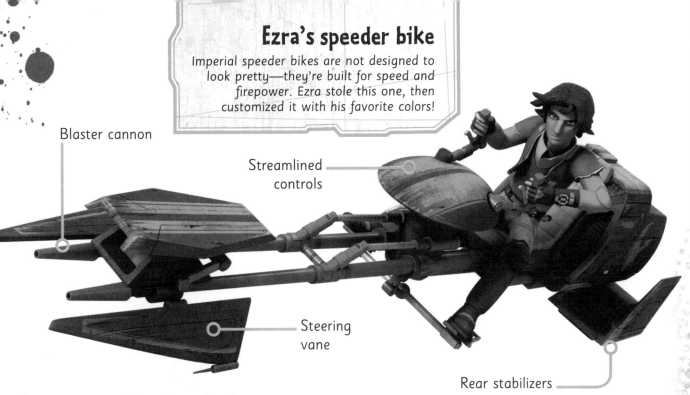

Blaster cannon

Streamlined controls

Steering vane

Rear stabilizers

My speeder bike is called a:

What **shape** is your speeder bike going to be?

What **colors** will you use on your speeder bike?

Does your speeder bike have **pedals** and **handlebars**?

Will your speeder bike have any **weapons**?

Imperial Posters
Wreck an Imperial poster

The Empire uses posters to make Imperial rule look powerful and impressive to the people of Lothal. The rebels take any opportunity to wreck these posters to show the Empire they are not afraid to stand up to it.

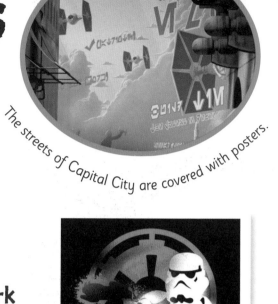

The streets of Capital City are covered with posters.

Learn about Imperial posters, then add some rebel touches to the one opposite.

Imperial icons

TIE fighters and stormtroopers are symbols of the Empire's power.

Dark symbol

The Imperial symbol features on all posters.

Recruitment posters

The Empire tries to recruit Lothal citizens to serve as stormtroopers. Posters are important tools for this.

Rebel tag

The rebels always leave behind their starbird symbol as a warning to the Empire.

For the Empire!

Simple, bold slogans are meant to persuade people.

A few improvements

The rebels hope that their "artwork" will convince people that the Empire is bad and will harm Lothal.

Find some **stickers** of the rebel starbird symbol at the back of the book.

Draw a **funny** face to make the stormtrooper look foolish.

Will you use **bright** colors to wreck the poster?

LONG LIVE THE EMPIRE!

Write the truth about the Empire across the Imperial message.

Chapter 3 Challenge
Test your knowledge of Chapter 3

Answer each question. If you need help, look back through the section.

Now you have finished the third chapter of the book, take the Challenge to prove your knowledge!

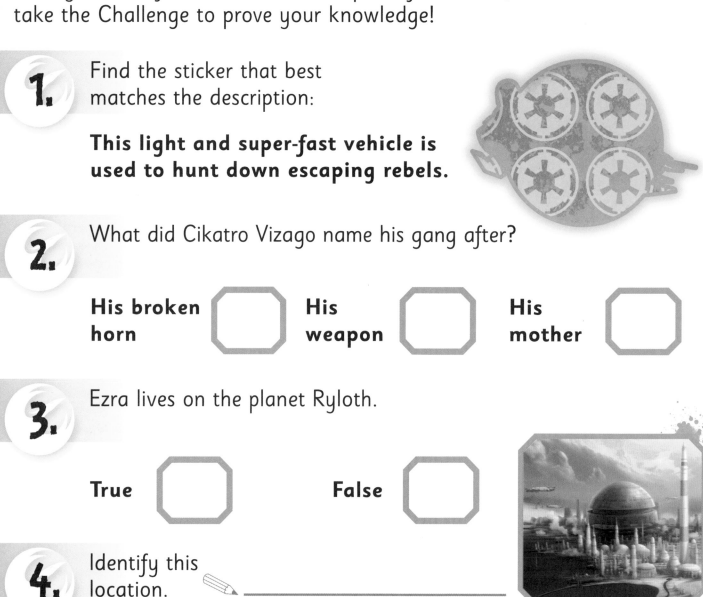

1. Find the sticker that best matches the description:

This light and super-fast vehicle is used to hunt down escaping rebels.

2. What did Cikatro Vizago name his gang after?

His broken horn ◯   **His weapon** ◯   **His mother** ◯

3. Ezra lives on the planet Ryloth.

True ◯   **False** ◯

4. Identify this location. ✎ _____

5. Ezra's ✎ _____ is a great place to keep an eye on the Empire.

Find the **answers** on page 97.

Now you have finished the Challenge, fill this scene with your extra stickers!

The rebels' missions against the Empire are incredibly dangerous. They could be captured by stormtroopers or blasted into dust by Imperial ships. But the rebels know that people are depending on them, so they bravely go on their missions.

Terrible traps

The Empire often sets traps to capture the rebels. But the rebels have become very good at escaping from them!

Fighting together

The rebels are a team. They fight the Empire together, and work to protect each other.

Find the **stickers** at the back of the book.

Explosive action

Sabine never goes on a mission without carrying a large amount of explosives with her.

Heroic Hera

Hera is not afraid of Imperial ships. She has flown the *Ghost* through hundreds of dogfights, and she always wins!

Rebel rescues

Prisoners of the Empire are shown no mercy. The rebels must try to save as many prisoners as they can.

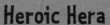

Jedi combat

Now that the Empire knows Kanan is a Jedi, he will be forced to use his Jedi abilities in battle a lot more often.

Helping people

The rebels want to help the people of Lothal. Whenever they can, they bring food to starving people or defend them against the Empire.

Bike Chase

Write in the speech bubbles

Street-smart Ezra can take care of himself and is always on the lookout for Imperial cargo to steal. But today, some strangers seem to be on the hunt for the same prize... Time for Ezra's first meeting with the rebels!

Decide what each character will say and write it in the blank speech bubbles.

You could write in **pencil** first and then use a **pen**.

Ezra steals a stormtrooper's speeder bike and zooms off with a crate.

Unknown to Ezra, rebels Kanan and Zeb are after the same booty...

Kanan and Zeb follow Ezra on their bikes, but he gets away!

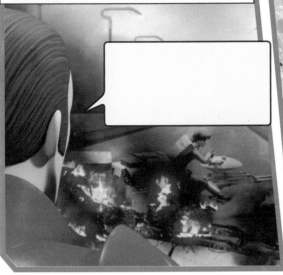

Boom! Imperial TIE fighters chase Ezra down and hit his bike with their lasers.

More TIE fighters are zooming through the sky. Ezra is trapped!

Suddenly, a spacecraft appears in the sky. Kanan tells Ezra to climb aboard.

Time has run out! Ezra makes a fast decision and leaps up onto the craft.

Piloting the Ghost

Complete the cockpit scene

The *Ghost* is the rebels' home. This special ship takes them wherever they need to go: from the dark depths of space, to the grasslands of Lothal, or into battle against the Empire.

The *Ghost* never lets the rebels down!

Draw the scene first, then **color it in**!

Look at these things that might be seen from the cockpit, then choose something to draw.

TIE fighters

Imperial TIE fighters are the *Ghost*'s most common enemy. These small, fast ships buzz around it like angry wasps, but the *Ghost* is one tough machine!

Deadly dogfights

When the rebels fight with Imperial ships, Hera easily outflies the Imperial pilots. The result is usually a big, fiery explosion!

The cockpit

The *Ghost*'s cockpit is not as cramped as some ships'. Hera normally sits in the pilot's seat to the left, while Kanan sits on the right.

Landscapes

The *Ghost* can land on any planet's surface. The cockpit gives a great view of the landscape and environment, whether it is desert, mountains, grasslands, or forests.

Hyperspace

When the *Ghost* enters hyperspace, the stars and blackness of space are replaced by a dazzling light show! Beautiful blue streaks zoom past the cockpit.

Lightsabers
Create a new lightsaber

Read about lightsabers, then design one of your own.

A Jedi apprentice must build their own lightsaber as one of the tests to become a Jedi. This means that no two lightsabers are the same, and that they are very personal to the one who made them.

The teacher

Anyone can use a lightsaber, but only Force-users can truly master one! Kanan learned his lightsaber skills from his old Jedi Master, Depa Billaba.

The student

Ezra has built his own lightsaber, but fighting without proper training is very dangerous. Kanan must train Ezra in all of the lightsaber arts.

Blue versus red

Evil Sith and other dark side warriors use lightsabers, too. Their lightsabers glow red instead of blue, and sometimes have two blades.

Ezra's lightsaber

Ezra's lightsaber is unusual. He built it out of spare junk that he found on board the *Ghost*. It has a blaster built into its handle.

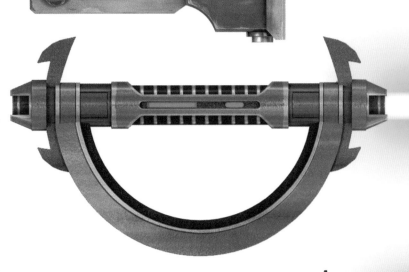

The Inquisitor's lightsaber

The Inquisitor's lightsaber has two blades and a unique spinning handle. It is a sinister-looking weapon, perfect for an evil warrior.

Kanan's lightsaber

Kanan's lightsaber is classic and simple; he built it when he was at the Jedi Temple. It can be broken into smaller pieces to make it easy to hide.

Draw your lightsaber **handle**.

What **shape** is your handle going to be?

Write about your lightsaber's **special features!**

Wookiee Rescue

Finish the comic strip

The rebels are going on a rescue mission! A tribe of Wookiees is being held prisoner by the Empire on the planet Kessel. If the rebels don't save them, they will be forced to work as slaves in the Empire's spice mines.

The Wookiees will not last long on Kessel.

Read the story, then write and draw the ending.

Use these images to help you.

Ezra

This is Ezra's first battle as one of the rebels. He will use his energy slingshot.

Kanan

If the rebels are going to escape, Kanan will have to use his Jedi powers.

Draw with a **pencil** before you use colored pens.

The Wookiee prisoners are being marched into the spice mines.

Move along! Keep moving!

The rebels land in the *Ghost* and rush into action.

Ezra! Get to the Wookiees!

Ezra manages to free the Wookiees from their binders.

Kanan takes his lightsaber and prepares for battle.

Agent Kallus is shocked! He thought the Jedi were extinct.

All troopers! Concentrate your fire on the Jedi!

Kanan must protect the Wookiees from Agent Kallus.

Wullffwarro

Wullffwarro is the leader of the Wookiee tribe. He is very big and strong.

Kitwarr

Kitwarr is Wullffwarro's son. He is the youngest and smallest member of the tribe.

Agent Kallus

Evil Agent Kallus wears black armor and a helmet that only shows his face.

Stormtroopers

The Wookiees are being guarded by a squad of Imperial stormtroopers.

How will the story **end**? You **decide**!

THE END!

Rebel Battles

Decide which rebel to send

The rebels each have special skills that they can use against the Empire. For every mission, Kanan has to come up with a plan that best uses their abilities. Good planning can be the difference between victory and defeat!

Read about the rebels and the missions. Then decide who Kanan should send on each mission and find the sticker showing what happens next.

Rebel general

As the rebels' commander, Kanan has to decide which rebels go on which missions. It can be a difficult decision—some missions are very dangerous!

Available rebels:

Ezra

Ezra is smart and brave. He hates injustice, and will fight to **free** anyone taken prisoner by the Empire.

Sabine

If something needs **blowing up**, Sabine is the one to send! Her explosives can destroy almost anything.

Zeb

Zeb is a master of close combat. If there are **stormtroopers** to deal with, Zeb is the perfect choice.

You can choose only **one rebel** for each mission, so decide **carefully**!

1 Defending civilians

Some stormtroopers are harrassing an innocent shopkeeper. They think that no one is brave enough to stand up to them. Who will Kanan send to teach them a lesson?

Kanan will send:

_____

What happens next:

2 Rescuing farmers

The Empire has taken these farmers prisoner and burned down their farm! Kanan will have to act fast if the rebels are going to free them. Who will he send to the rescue?

Kanan will send:

_____

What happens next:

3 Sabotaging TIE fighters

TIE fighters are easier to destroy when they are on the ground. Someone will need to sneak into this Imperial base and place some explosives. Who will Kanan send?

Kanan will send:

_____

What happens next:

Find the **stickers** at the back of the book.

Find the **answers** on page 97.

Battling the Inquisitor

Find the missing stickers

The rebels must fight many scary enemies, but the most dangerous enemy of all is the Inquisitor. Quick, intelligent, and merciless, this Imperial menace uses the dark side of the Force to defeat his foes.

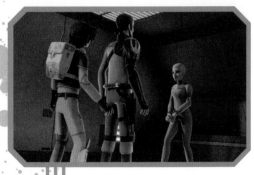

The rebels are on a secret mission in the Spire. Kanan and Ezra break into a cell to **rescue a captive Jedi Master**.

Read about the duel, then use the clues to find the missing stickers.

Oh no—it's a trap! A menacing stranger appears, with **gray skin and high-collared armor**. It's the Inquisitor!

The Spire

The Empire's most powerful enemies are held in the Spire—a dark, sinister prison on a remote planet.

Dark side warrior

The Inquisitor analyzes his foes' fighting styles, to exploit their weaknesses. He also summons the power of the dark side.

Brave but rusty

Kanan uses precise jabs and blocks. However, his incomplete training means he cannot match the Inquisitor.

Find the **answers** on page 97.

The Inquisitor attacks Kanan with his **red lightsaber**. The Jedi fights back with his **blue one** and a **fierce duel** begins.

The Inquisitor easily **blocks Kanan's blows with his blade**. **Kanan is shocked** to find out his Jedi skills are no match for this foe.

The evil villain knocks Kanan over with a **flying kick in the back**. Ezra fires stun-balls with his slingshot, but the Inquisitor is unharmed.

Ezra uses a **thermal detonator bomb** to create a distraction. The rebels grab their chance to escape and run down the corridor.

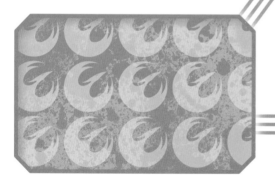

The Inquisitor is hot on their heels. Ezra watches in horror as he **attacks**, revealing his deadly lightsaber has **two blades**!

The Inquisitor uses a Force-push to throw Kanan through the air. Luckily, Kanan and Ezra escape again. They **flee the prison with the other rebels**.

The Inquisitor won't let them get away. He puts his lightsaber into **spinning mode** and **throws** it at the rebels.

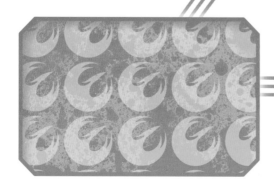

Kanan manages to block the spinning weapon. The rebels jump into the *Phantom* and **fly away to safety**.

Find the **stickers** at the back of the book.

Chapter 4 Challenge
Test your knowledge of Chapter 4

Answer each question. If you need help, look back through the section.

Now you have finished the fourth chapter of the book, take the Challenge and show you are ready to join the rebels!

1. Find the sticker that best matches the description:

This spaceship is the rebels' home. It is one tough machine!

2. Which one of these is an Imperial prison?

The Rock 　　**The Pinnacle** 　　**The Spire**

3. Kanan is the rebels' explosives expert.

True 　　**False**

4. What are these Imperial soldiers known as? _____

5. A tribe of Wookiees is being held prisoner on the planet _____ .

Find the **answers** on page 97.